THE LITTLE ART BOOK

edited by BERTHOLD FRICKE

KURT MARTIN

THE ALTE PINAKOTHEK
IN MUNICH

TRANSLATED FROM THE GERMAN
BY STANLEY GODMAN
AND IAN F. FINLAY

KNORR & HIRTH VERLAG GMBH
D-3167 AHRBECK/HANNOVER

All rights, in particular of translation and reproduction, reserved. The firm of SCHRÖER & CO. *at Seelze, was responsible for the setting and printing,* SIGLOCH *at Künzelsau/Württemberg for the binding;* A. GÄSSLER & CO. LTD. *of Munich, for the block making, and* JOACHIM BLAUEL *of Munich for the colour photographs. Printed in Germany. A large volume in the series "The Little Art Book", edited by* BERTHOLD FRICKE.

© KNORR & HIRTH VERLAG GMBH
1968, 1972 & 1976

Introduction

The history of the Bavarian art collections covers a period of over 400 years in which, spared by good fortune from the ravages of war, pillage, accident and human folly, it was possible for them to build up their present world-wide fame. They owe their quality to the taste and determination of the ardent collectors and connoisseurs who flowed in a continual stream from the House of Wittelsbach. Their development was also assisted by the fact that, when the Bavarian line died out in 1771, the Palatine branch of the family and, after its extinction, the Palatine-Zweibrücken line came to power in Bavaria. The celebrated collections of Düsseldorf, Mannheim and Carlsberg Castle near Homburg on the Saar were for this reason transferred to Munich at the beginning of the 19th century and combined with the already existing rich collection. Secularisation brought a further important increment from episcopal collections, churches and monasteries. Considerable purchases were also made by the Crown Prince and later King Ludwig I, to whose generous initiative and planning Munich owes its modern face. Apart from important single works, the famous collections of early German and early Netherlandish paintings belonging to the Boisserée brothers and Prince von Öttingen-Wallerstein were acquired. There came into being a gallery of the highest quality and considerable size in which, unlike museums whose aim is to provide a well-balanced survey of the history of art and a complete historical conspectus, even today the personalities of the outstanding collectors can still be clearly discerned in the various sections. Examples of this may be seen in the unique wealth of masterpieces by Rubens, in what is probably the most comprehensive collection of early German painting, with special emphasis on Dürer, in the great number of paintings by van Dyck and Jan Brueghel the Elder, in the series of pictures by Rembrandt — early works such as the 18th century preferred — in the broad display of Dutch "schilderkonst", and also in the outstanding representation of the Italian painting of the Renaissance, above all of Titian and Raphael, and finally in the important works of Roger van der Weyden, Poussin, Claude Lorrain and Murillo.

In order to contain the wealth that it was impossible to accommodate in the old Electoral gallery in the pavilion of the Hofgarten, it was necessary to build a new museum. Ludwig I (who reigned from 1825 to 1848) found in Leo von Klenze (1784—1864) the architect who was able to give the conception a form which provided a model for the whole of the 19th century and is still valid today. The Old Pinakothek was built — and this is characteristic of the boldness of the town-planning conception — outside the city gates, almost in the open country, and was opened to the public on October 16, 1836.

The succeeding decades, especially from 1875 onwards, served to round off and replenish the collection. The many important acquisitions included early German panels, paintings by Antonello da Messina, Pieter Brueghel the Elder, Goya, Greco, Guardi, Leonardo, Frans Hals and Rembrandt.

There was above all the need to extend the collection to the present age. Between 1846 and 1853 there was built, on a site north of the Old Pinakothek, the New Pinakothek which was devoted to 19th century painting. Since 1927 the New State Gallery on the Königs-platz, which was built between 1838 and 1845 for temporary exhibitions, has been devoted to modern art.

All these buildings were much damaged in the second world war. The Old Pinakothek, the reconstruction of which was made possible mainly by voluntary contributions, was re-opened on June 7, 1957. Since then the main story has been open to visitors, as before. A necessary extension that has been under discussion on and off for over 50 years is to be attained by the development of the ground floor where since 1961 the section devoted to "German and Dutch painting between the Renaissance and the Baroque" has been on view and where the section "German Painting of the 15th century" is opened since 1963. Comprehensive plans for an up-to-date rebuilding are under way for the New Pinakothek and the New State Gallery, whose collections are provisionally on exhibition in the west wing of the "House of Art".

No artist of his period attained such far-reaching influence on his contemporaries and the younger generation as Roger van der Weyden, not only in the Netherlands but also in France and Spain, and even in Italy, and in particular measure in Germany. The main reason for his influence was his ability decisively to mould the expression of his age. After the loving surrender to Nature and the absorption in the wealth and manifold wonders of this world which were so characteristic of the Van Eyck brothers, Roger brought art back to the devout representation of ecclesiastical subjects.

Roger's splendid austerity is shown in his renunciation of all the charms of mere chance. The space is always clearly demarcated, even when the illusion is created of successively receding vistas and views. No less definite are the figures, standing not in, but in front of the space occupied by the picture. It is possible to sense the flesh behind the richly expressive folds and colours of the garments, but it has no physical weight. Great importance is attached to the composition, to the unity of a meeting or a confrontation. For all its wealth and all its splendour, for all its radiance and beauty, the colour is only intended to convey cool effects. Roger abandoned the fullness of life and through the power of his personality lifted the reality of earth up into the world of piety and faith. This, and not merely the outstanding quality of his art, is the reason for the example which he set.

The hovering entrance of the angel, the shy and gentle Mary, her raised hand, with which she accompanies the tender intrusion of the Annunciation — how perfect in itself is this portrayal and how far above all human utterance! The Presentation in the Temple is impressive by reason of the lucid variety of the ecclesiastical interior, the account of the action is entirely objective and striving precisely thereby to do justice to the symbolical nature of the episode.

The German painter who migrated to the Netherlands to complete his training or to absorb new impressions, already encountered our Altarpiece of the Kings in Cologne, which was at that time one of Europe's great and leading cities. A masterpiece of Roger's late period, it was created in 1460, or shortly before, for the chapel in St. Columba established by Goddert van den Wasservass.

1. ROGER VAN DER WEYDEN
or ROGIER DE LA PASTURE
born in 1399 or 1400 in Tournai and died on June 16, 1464 in Brussels.

THE ALTARPIECE OF THE THREE KINGS
Middle panel: The Adoration of the Magi, oakwood, 138 by 153 cm; left wing: The Annunciation, oakwood, 138 x 70 cm; right wing: The Presentation in the Temple, oakwood, 138 x 70 cm; no pictures on the reverse; from the collection of the Boisserée brothers.

The veneration of the "Joys of Mary", by which is meant a varying number of events in the life of the Madonna, reaches back into the 12th century. In the end it was agreed to concentrate on seven of the joys, though Memling did not rigidly adhere to them.

He extends his description wherever feasible and shows the town of Bethlehem set in a wide landscape, in order to obtain the space for the various subjects with their various localities. In this way it was possible to combine their diversity in a spatial unity. This enabled Memling to adorn the story with detailed secondary scenes. The more he gets away from the sacred element, the more unaffected the representation becomes. The star of Bethlehem appears to the Kings, they visit Herod, who has just ordered the killing of the innocent babes. They travel through the countryside to reach their goal and adore the Child. The picture also contains a detailed account of the return journey: a group of attendants, including two Moors on camels, has already set out and is just riding into a narrow pass; one of them is quickly mounting his horse to catch up with the others. Such observations are a proof of Memling's sense of reality and feeling for the natural, which he reproduces with amiable precision.

According to a reliable account the original frame of the picture, which has not survived, contained an inscription in Flemish:

"In the year 1480 this work was donated to the Tanner's Guild by Mr. Pieter Bultynk, the son of Joost, tanner and merchant, and of his wife Katharina, the daughter of Gottfried von Riebecke, and the brothers of the Guild are to read a Miserere and a De Profundis for all the deceased after every mass." The chapel of the Tanners was in the church of our Lady in Bruges.

2. HANS MEMLING
born circa 1433, probably in Mömm-lingen near Mainz, died in Bruges on August 11, 1494.

THE SEVEN JOYS OF MARY
(section: the Procession of the Kings), oakwood, 81 x 189 cm. From the collection of the Boisserée brothers.

The small altar comes from the domestic chapel of the Snoy family in Malines and was by reason of its exquisite painting rightly called the "Pearl of Brabant". It was regarded as a work of Dirk Bouts the Elder (born circa 1420 in Haarlem, died on May 6, 1475 in Louvain), who seemed to be nearest to it in style. It was then found, however, that our little altar, with a number of other pictures, should, on account of the "greater degree of elegance in the formal pattern and the choice of gay and glowing colours", be conceived as the work of a younger artist, to whom was given the name of the "Master of the Pearl of Brabant". To solve the enigma of his anonymity, attempts have been made, with good reason, to identify him with Dirk Bouts the Younger, who is thought to have been a painter (born around 1448—1450, died in Louvain between December 28, 1490 and May 2, 1491), though no documented work has come down to us. The master responsible for this picture is in command of the whole of his artistic inheritance, seizes hold of it with great vivacity and endows it with the unprecedented radiance of his glowing colours. Thanks to its immaculate state of preservation, the impact that this perfect painting makes on the beholder is one of immediate and unmixed joy.

3. THE MASTERS OF THE "PEARL OF BRABANT" *was active in the 2nd half of the 15th century in the Netherlands.*

SMALL ALTARPIECE WITH WINGS *known as the "Pearl of Brabant". Centre panel: Adoration of the Magi, left wing inner side: John the Baptist in a Landscape; outer side: St. Catharine (grisaille); right wing inner side: St. Christopher carries the Christ Child through the river; outer side: St. Barbara (grisaille); oakwood, centre panel 63 x 62 cm, each wing 63 x 28 cm. From the collection of the Boisserée brothers.*

The small panel with the "Adoration of the Child" by Stefan Lochner, one of the best known and most sensitive pictures of the Nativity in German art, is entirely permeated by the purity of a mystic imagination. The beginning is confronted with the end: the reverse portrays the Crucifixion, with Mary and John. In all probability this "Adoration of the Child" is a companion-piece to a picture of the same size dated 1445 with the "Presentation in the Temple" and the "Stigmatisation of St. Francis" on the reverse side. It is not certain whether they formed the wings of a small house altar or were two panels from some other context.

This Adoration was already regarded as a model by Lochner's own contemporaries. Thus the Masson collection in the Ecole Nationale Supérieure des Beaux-Arts in Paris contains a drawing of Mary, essentially a garment study, which probably derived from the master's immediate circle. And the British Museum contains a drawing after the picture in which the figure of the Virgin is reproduced in detail, the Christ child and the shepherds are merely indicated, and the stable and landscape are missing. Finally, the Cologne "Master of the Heisterbach altar" freely reproduced the scene in a panel of his main work (Bavarian State Collections).

Blue is Mary's symbolic colour. Here it dominates the whole picture, a cool, radiant blue enveloping the maidenly, almost childlike Mary and removing her from her earthly surroundings. And there is another blue, of a different quality, in the garments and wings of the angels, in the trio that looks down from the stable window on to the child Jesus lying on the ground, in the quartet that sings the Gloria among the roof beams, and finally in the angel hovering down from heaven, to proclaim the joyful tidings to the shepherds. How like a jewel is this colour, how precious the brightness of this night, in whose radiance the moon turns pale!

Mary's heartfelt abandonment to adoration is not lacking in signs of that which is to come. Not only the saving Child lies within her sight, but also the little cloth, embroidered with crosses, which is its bed. May that not be intended to suggest a communion cloth and hence refer to the Master's sacrificial death and the holy sacrifice of the mass? In this picture there is a plainly religious joy in the way the natural is extended beyond the dimension of beauty and serves to illuminate the miracle in a complete harmony of colour, form and composition.

4. STEFAN LOCHNER
born presumably between 1405 and 1415 in Meersburg on Lake Constance, died in Cologne between September 22 and December 24, 1451.

THE ADORATION OF THE CHILD
on the reverse: The Crucifixion, oakwood, 36 x 23 cm, acquired in 1961.

The master acquired his reputation from the paintings of an extensive altar of the Virgin that was made for St. Ursula's in Cologne. The story of the Virgin Mary is told on 8 panels, of which 7 are now in the Old Pinakothek. The paintings were arranged in two layers, showing in the upper series: the meeting at the Golden Gate, the birth of Mary, her walk to the Temple and her marriage; and in the lower series: the Annunciation, the Visitation, the Presentation in the Temple (National Gallery, London) and the Assumption. When the wings were closed it was also possible to see the Crucifixion and the crowning of Mary.

The story begins in the background. After having been turned out of the Temple "because thou art sterile", Joachim is far away in the fields with his servants and animals. In the second scene an angel commands him to go home: "When thou comest to the Golden Gate, thy hostess Anna will meet you." The angel had also appeared to her and prophesied that despite her age she would bear a child. He had also bidden her hasten to the Golden Gate.

These three groups, which are accompanied by the slender towers of the gates of Jerusalem, are interrelated by a peculiarly restrained rhythm. The carefulness of the portrayal, the restraint in all the movements, is in accord with the nature of the art of Cologne and the personality of the Master who took Dirk Bouts as his first model but was also influenced by Roger van der Weyden, whose painting was so to say daily before his eyes in Cologne, in the church of St. Columba, for which he himself made the high altar. Compared with the elegance of the Dutch painter's execution, the suppleness of these forms and the splendour of the colour, the panels of the Master of the Life of Mary seem bourgeois and naïve, more modest in their formal development and colour. On the other hand, the narratives are carefully decorated and full of a genuinely intimate feeling. The panels of this Altar of the Virgin probably derive from the beginning of the seventies of the 15th century.

5. THE MASTER
OF THE LIFE OF THE VIRGIN
active in Cologne between 1450 and 1480.

THE MEETING AT THE GOLDEN GATE
oakwood, 85 x 106 cm, from the collection of the Boiserée brothers.

When the altar is opened out, the four great fathers of the church are revealed: Hieronymus, Augustine, Gregory and Ambrose, of whom Hieronymus and Ambrose are portrayed on the inner sides of the wings. On the outer sides Pacher painted four scenes from the legend of St. Wolfgang, which give the view of the closed altar. The predella (altar step) on which probably the usual subject of Christ with the twelve apostles was depicted, the original framework and the strutframe, which all added to the total effect of the work, have not survived.

Hieronymus, to whom we owe the Vulgate translation of the Bible into Latin, which is still in general use today, is engaged in removing with his penknife a painful thorn from the paw of a lion which has trustingly approached him. Ambrose is about to write and is just trying out his pen. He is joined by a child in a cradle: a reference to the legend according to which the cry of a child was decisive in his election as bishop of Milan.

The saints are sitting in complicated pews with canopies decorated with crabs and little pointed turrets in which statues are standing. These manifold details all serve to heighten the effect of space which permeates everything and give the pictures a new unity of their own. The way the cradle and the almost doll-like child are shaped recalls the fact that Pacher was a sculptor, and that he owed much to Italian influence, especially the art of Mantegna which he assimilated without surrendering his own tradition. There is a peculiar tension in the picture, with its overwhelming grandeur and significance, to which the refined movements and finely articulated decoration make their essential contribution.

6. MICHAEL PACHER
born about 1435 near or in Neustift near Brixen (Bressanone), died on August 24, 1489, probably in Bruneck (Brunico).

THE ALTARPIECE
OF THE FATHERS OF THE CHURCH
stone-pine wood, centre panel, 216 by 196 cm, wings each 206 x 91 cm; 1812 from Neustift monastery near Brixen.

When the 21 year-old Dürer arrived on his travels in 1492 in Kolmar, Schongauer with whom he hoped to continue his studies had already died. He was acquainted with copper engravings by him, these being widely spread at the time and serving artists in Germany and elsewhere as a stimulus and model. It is an ancient tradition that the young Michelangelo copied the sheet with the Temptation of St. Anthony, while an engraving of the carrying of the cross was copied in details by Memlinc, Dürer and Raphael. While we possess an extensive collection of works from the field of the graphic arts by Schongauer — these being alongside those of Dürer, Rembrandt and Goya artistically the most important in Europe — a few paintings only by him have come down to us. These are, above all, "May in the Rose-Grove" (1473) in St. Martin in Kolmar, which has been called "the German Sistine Madonna", as well as a few small panels, including the "Holy Family" in Munich.

The very girlish madonna of our picture is sitting on a grassy seat in front of the ruined cowshed and holding the new-born baby, whom she is supporting carefully, on her lap. She is showing him with dainty fingers a blue flower she has just picked from the chicory plant at her side, this resulting in an admittedly insignificant, yet very natural connexion between her and her surroundings. Perhaps its importance in warding off disaster led to the choice of this plant, possibly however it is intended merely to evoke the colour blue which was in the Middle Ages connected with the mother of God and required for the representation.

Mary's charming figure which dominates the picture is fully occupied with herself and her happiness. She is, as it were, connected with the rest of the story merely from the point of view of the composition. There is the cowshed with its roof of straw which has been pierced by the weather and the supports and beams of which not only characterize the poverty of the spot, but at the same time form an essential framework for the composition. When we learn that, according to the original laying-out of the picture, the building was intended to extend further to the left, it is easy to verify what the picture gained in compactness and clarity of construction through this correction. It shows clearly with what intention the madonna, whose head stands out so clearly from the dark background, has been moved from the centre of the picture.

We have in addition the ox and the donkey with their so very characteristic animal expressions and, in particular, Joseph the provider who, as had been suggested, in no way plays a somewhat wretched rôle and moves in an embarrassed way from one foot to the other, but is just stepping over the threshold and reaching for his stick. The blue of his robe and the red

7. MARTIN SCHONGAUER
born in about 1435 in Augsburg and died on February 2, 1491 in Breisach.

THE HOLY FAMILY
painted between 1475 and 1480, lime wood, 26 x 17 cm. Taken over from the Zweibrücken Gallery.

OSWOLT·KREL
1499

of the cloth which he has slung around his head after the manner of a turban are balanced by the red of Mary's dress which attains its full effect only through this harmonic supplementation. In the background, hilly meadows rise up above the blue water of a pond, in addition to rocks, a wooded knoll and a distant blue mountain-range — all in all a sober picture of nature below a high and calm sky.

Such small panels painted with the finest of brushes served for personal edification and private devotion.

8. ALBRECHT DÜRER
born on May 21, 1471 in Nuremberg, died on April 6, 1528 in Nuremberg.

PORTRAIT OF OSWOLT KREL
signed Oswolt Krel 1499, lime tree wood, 50 x 39 cm; from the collection of Prince von Öttingen-Wallerstein.

When Dürer painted this portrait, he was 28 years old. His patron, a rich merchant, came from a Lindau family; he occupied the important post of manager of the Ravensburg trading company which controlled a considerable part of the commerce between West Germany and Italy and maintained relations with countries in the Northern parts of Europe. He was one of the type created by early capitalism, energetic and enterprising, and prepared to use and exploit the economic power which had been placed in his hands.

But Dürer was also a member of the younger generation. He was at this time engaged on the series of woodcuts on the Apocalypse, with their passionate formal language. He now applied his heightened sense of life to the portrayal of man. It is no longer merely a question of simply copying human features; what is required now is an understanding of the individual and a new sense of commitment to man and Nature. There is therefore a feeling of tension and excitement in the features and look of this man, which is not a momentary emotion but the expression of a new self-consciousness.

Two little panels (49.3 x 15.9 and 49.7 x 15.7 cm, Old Pinakothek) served as a protection for this portrait, though it is not known exactly how they were connected with it. The arms of Oswolt Krel and his wife Agathe von Esendorf were portrayed, held up by "Wild men".

"I Albrecht Dürer from Nuremberg have represented myself in this way, with the colours which are characteristic of me, at the age of 28." Thus reads the inscription. We know what Dürer looked like from numerous painted and drawn self-portraits. None has touched and engaged posterity so much and has become so famous as that of the Munich Pinakothek. It has up till today been the one to stamp the idea of this his personality.

By this pure frontal view, symmetry of construction, stressing of the vertical element, renunciation of a three-dimensional effect, seriousness and the fixed nature of the expression, Dürer has conferred upon himself a solemnity which borders on the hieratic. This is increased by the constant, open look which does not ask and seek, but is directed calmly and inescapably straight at the observer. There is, in addition, the artistically waved and plaited hair and the graceful and well-groomed beard. The individual element with all its coincidences has been overcome in favour of an idealization which unmistakably reminds one of the head of a Salvator mundi or "Saviour of the World". The hand which is full of character and which feels sensitively at the fox fur of the fashionable houppelande likewise appears to have been animated by a gesture of blessing.

Up till then, no person had seen and dared to depict himself in this way. We should consequently not be surprised that this highly important portrait has always exerted an attracting and gripping, but also disturbing effect. What might Dürer's intention have been, when the 28 year-old artist painted himself in this way, present only in timelessness and with a dignity which seems to border on the religious? We possess from him too many testimonies of deepest piety and christian humility so that we can exclude any thought of blasphemy or vanity. It has also been said that he did not represent himself as he estimated himself as an artist, but as he strove to be. Above all however, around about 1500, i.e. at the same time as this self-portrait was painted, Dürer began to study proportions which could be measured and calculated, and thus arrived from an intuitively determined to an intellectually controlled view of his art. Efforts have therefore been made to show that a rationally acquired construction considered in this sense lay at the basis of our self-portrait, such as in fact applies to many later representations of human beings and horses, this also having been substantiated by Dürer in detail in theoretical studies. The laws of proportion contained, according to the view in his time, the secret of the beautiful, of harmony and thus of perfection, in fact what, as people believed, held the secret to creation.

9. ALBRECHT DÜRER
born on May 21, 1471 in Nuremberg and died on April 6, 1528 in Nuremberg.

SELF-PORTRAIT
marked at the top left: "1500 AD", at the top right the inscription: "ALBERTUS DURERUS NORICUS / IPSUM ME PROPRIIS SIC EFFIN. / GEBAM COLORIBUS AETATIS / ANNO XXVIII". Lime wood, 67 x 49 cm. Formerly in the Nuremberg Townhall, purchased from a private collection in 1805.

Dürer dit not give the "Four Apostles" to a church, but presented them in June 1526 to the Council of Nuremberg, his native city, exhorting them to remain true to the new Faith. "All secular rulers in these dangerous times must watch lest they are seduced by man rather than following the word of God. God does not desire anything to be added to His word or to be taken from it. Hear therefore the warning of those excellent men Peter, John, Paul and Mark" — thus begins the inscription at the foot of the figures, which continues with quotations from the New Testament. In this work Dürer made a personal profession of faith in Luther and the Reformation which had been introduced in Nuremberg in 1525; at the same time he was attacking all false prophets and sectarians, of whom there was no lack in Nuremberg and even in his own personal circle.

The two panels are reminiscent of the wings of an altar and derive from the tradition of the medieval altar. The omission of a picture in the centre means that a new content as well a new form is obtained. It has been rightly pointed out that the true centre has now been taken by the spiritual importance of the inscriptions. The definition of the subject is secured by the world of the messengers of the Faith. The power which Dürer gave to his figures is not derived from the holiness bestowed on them by the Roman church but from a dicision for the Faith and the Protestant confession. This is suggested not only by their statuesque attitude and the concentrated energy of their expression but equally by the inward greatness of the form and the clarity of the colour. The moral demand inherent in the "Four Apostles" is in the art itself. In these panels Dürer concentrated all his human and artistic experience, applying to them "more diligence than to other paintings". They are his finest achievement.

10. ALBRECHT DÜRER
born in Nuremberg on May 21, 1471, died in Nuremberg on April 6, 1528.

"THE FOUR APOSTLES":
John and Peter, signed with the monogram and the date 1526, Paul and Mark, lime wood, 214 x 76 and 214.5 x 76 cm. Left to the Elector Maximilian I by the Nuremberg Town Council.

Grünewald was commissioned to paint the panel of Erasmus and Maurice by Cardinal Albrecht of Brandenburg, the most powerful church prince of this time, who when he was only 24 already united under his mitre the bishopric of Halberstadt, the archbishopric of Magdeburg and the archbishopric of Mainz, which was also of the highest rank and with which the chancellorship of the Reich was combined. The picture was intended for the altar of St. Maurice in the church of the charitable institution at Halle which had been newly founded by Albrecht and which he had in a short time extravagantly provided with no less than 353 precious reliquaries. These included an over-lifesize silver statue of St. Maurice which Grünewald took as the model for his picture. For St. Erasmus, who is recognisable by the winch used to wrench his intestines from his body at his martyrdom, Albrecht demanded the faithful reproduction of his own person in the official robes, bedecked with pearls and gold and precious stones, which he wore at pontifical high mass. The Bishop's crosier was among the treasures of Magdeburg Cathedral. The Cardinal was not merely indulging in personal vanity and a thirst for glory. Identifying oneself with saints was in line with the general secularisation of the time.

Erasmus and Maurice are engaged in a lively conversation. They are accompanied, to a certain extent on a second plane, by an old Canon and a crossbow man of the Theban legion, who by their arrangement in the picture offset the striking displacement of the main group. The freedom of the exposition shows how far in this late work of circa 1521 Grünewald had freed himself from all medieval con eptions: the perfection and preciousness of the painting have never been attained again in German art.

11. GRÜNEWALD
(MATHIS GOTHARDT NEITHARDT, *called* GRÜNEWALD)
probably born between 1475 and 1480 (but, according to some, around 1460) in Würzburg, died in Halle on August 28 or 29, 1528.

THE SAINTS ERASMUS AND MAURICE IN CONVERSATION
lime wood, 226 x 176 cm. Taken over from the Aschaffenburg Gallery in 1836.

12. LUCAS CRANACH THE ELDER
(LUCAS MALER, *called*)
born in Cronach in Upper Franconia in October 1472, died in Weimar on October 16, 1553.

MADONNA AND CHILD
signed with the master sign (serpent with upright wings), beech wood, 60 x 24 cm. Presented by King Maximilian I in 1824.

One of Cranach's several pictures of the Virgin Mary, the half-figure of the Madonna. She is handing to the naked child standing on a cushion a bunch of grapes from which it has plucked a berry that it is trying to put in its Mother's mouth. In this extremely human relationship is laid the religious meaning of the picture which is otherwise suggested only by the type of painting and by the angels who are spreading out a purple material behind the Madonna. The cloth opens up a view across a wooded hill to a fortified rock, into a river valley and to distant mountains. It is the mood of the landscape rather than its spatial setting that connects it with the content of the picture. This picture which was definitely painted by the artist himself, dates from about 1520, before the inordinate production of Cranach's workshop had begun.

Mary is enthroned, with the Child on her lap, in the clouds, surrounded by the angelic hosts who fill the sky with their "Gloria in excelsis". These are no grown-up, stern and serious angels, but joyful music-making little children. The Madonna faces the faithful who, then as now, are blessed by the child. Over her head two hovering putti hold the crown, which denotes the rank of the Queen of heaven. The eternal being of her person rests in the infinity of this heaven where her halo shines like a sun.

Altdorfer enshrines the Holy in a cosmic vision, in clouds and light, in distances beyond our ken, and peoples them with myriads of angels. At the feet of the Madonna, under the ribbon of cloud, an earthly landscape with lakes and distant mountains extends in a calm passivity on which the light of evening rests. The "Mary in the Angel's Halo" dates from about 1525 and marks the beginning of Altdorfer's final and richest phase, which was to reach its climax in the "Battle of Alexander" of 1529 (cp. No. 14).

13. ALBRECHT ALTDORFER
*born shortly before 1480, possibly in Regensburg (Ratisbon), **died on February 12, 1538 in Regensburg**.*

MADONNA AND CHILD
IN THE ANGEL'S HALO
signed with the monogram. On the reverse: Mary Magdalene at Christ's Tomb, signed with the monogram. Lime wood, 66 x 43 cm. 1803 from Neuburg castle on the Danube.

14. ALBRECHT ALTDORFER
born shortly before 1480, possibly in Regensburg, died on February 12, 1538 in Regensburg (Ratisbon).

THE VICTORY OF ALEXANDER
the Great over the king of the Persians Darius III at the battle of Issus in 333 B. C. Signed on the lower edge of the frame of the inscription tablet: "Albrecht Altdorfer zu Regensburg fecit". At the bottom left the monogram AA and the year 1529. Lime wood, 158.4 by 120.3 cm.

In 1528 Duke William IV of Bavaria commissioned the city painter of Regensburg, Albrecht Altdorfer, to paint a representation of the battle of Issus, this being intended, together with 15 other secular and religious stories, for decorating his residence in the Munich "Neuveste". Altdorfer, who had just been elected burgomaster, took his task so seriously that he requested a dispensation from this obligation. The council granted him this by way of great exception only.

The subject of the battle of Issus, in which the youthful Alexander decisively conquered the Persians under Darius III and liberated Europe for centuries from the threat from Asia, was stimulated from the humanist side. It was at the time of Altdorfer particularly topical. In 1453 Constantinople fell, in 1521 the Turks conquered Belgrade, in 1522 Rhodes had to surrender, being the last foothold of Christianity in the East, while war had raged in Hungary since 1526 and, in 1529, the enemy stood before Vienna.

We know the ancient tradition which was available at the time: the "Historia Alexandri Magni" by Qu. Curtius Rufus, which Erasmus had edited in 1514 and dedicated to the brother of Duke William, and the "Anabasis Alexandri" by Flavius Arrianus, which Emperor Sigismund had translated from Greek into Latin. The "Bavarian Plutarch", Johannes Aventinus, from whom Altdorfer possibly received the historical data for his picture, had based his work in particular on that of Curtius.

Since there was no knowledge and conception of antiquity, history could be understood merely within the framework and area of the present and by the experiences of the contemporary age. The battle therefore takes place in a German landscape. Issus is a mediaeval European city with churches instead of temples. The knights of Maximilian enter the lists against one another, clad and armed according to that period.

Altdorfer does not enter into the depiction of individual actions of the battle and thus avoids any anecdotal representation. He sees the totality of the battle, the movement of the armies surging to and fro, which expresses the uncertain nature of the result, the crowd and bustle of the warriors, the tempestuous advance in the centre and the first turning to flight. He catches the eventful character of the incident such as no-one had done before him or probably has after him either. He achieves this because he has chosen an elevated vantage-point from which the development of the battle can be surveyed with almost geographical accuracy and objectivity. Only in this way has it been possible for the artist to convey the impression of a mass action with the innumerable, miniature-like small figures, without ever sliding off into the pedantic.

The decision is reached in the midst of the tumult. Alexander dashes forward with couched lance at the head of his selected men against his royal opponent. Yet Darius does not accept the fight. His war-chariot is already turned in flight. He realizes with a painful look the force and power of Alexander at the mercy of which he inevitably is.

This human drama is embedded in the wide expanse of the event and in natural surroundings which extend over hills, a strait and islands to the distant snowy mountain-ranges, a world landscape which reposes alone and magnificently in itself, untouched by all that is human and historical. Above it is the arch of a sky with the powerfully setting sun which breaks the clouds above the horizon and gilds their edges, a cosmic event from eternity to eternity which absorbs and irradiates the historical significance of the battle for the world.

Since the panels belong together, the subjects must also be connected with one another. Hence the traditional descriptions are not really adequate. It has recently been suggested that the two figures represent a confrontation of the passive temperaments, the so-called "Music" being the phlegmatic and the "Vanitas" the melancholic. The "Music" with the white cat would in this case be under the influence of the planet Venus, patroness of music and love. The serpent and also the stag, which can be made out in the background, are attributes of Prudentia, though the victory over the serpent cannot be derived directly from the Biblical saying, "Be ye wise as serpents". The Prudentia corresponds to the melancholy temperament and comes under Saturn. Perhaps, in order to complete the series, Baldung painted or intended to paint two further pictures, depicting the active temperaments, the sanguine and the choleric.

Such allegories evoke dark powers and forces, new knowledge and influences which Baldung adopted uneasily. His nudes are conceived with barely controlled sensuality, almost over-emphasized, and therefore the more appropriate for this type of picture. The unreality of the effect is stressed by the rigorous contrasts between light and dark; the uncertainty as to where the figures are actually standing heightens the feeling of mystery and this, combined as it is with an exact portrayal of the material objects, intensifies the impact of the picture as a whole. The two pictures bear witness to an age which was familiar with the figure of Dr. Faustus.

15. HANS BALDUNG-GRIEN
born in 1484 in Schwäbisch-Gmünd, died in 1545 in Strasbourg.

"MUSICA" *and* "VANITAS"
both panels signed with the monogram, and the so-called "Vanitas" also with the date 1529. Firwood, each 83 x 36 cm. Since 1799 in the Court Garden Gallery in Munich.

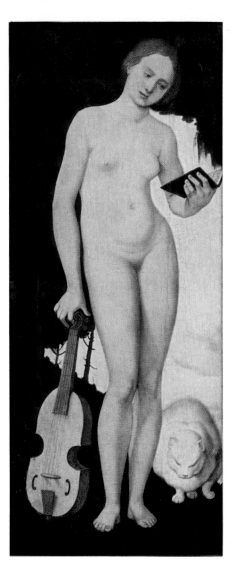

Elsheimer did not paint any picture from nature, but he was so inspired by and imbued with nature that she passed almost automatically into his art. He is depicted as a quiet, introvert person, always ready to absorb and to explain and heighten his impressions, who only stepped in front of his easel when an inner compulsion required him to, and then painted for a long time carefully at his small pictures. His work is meagre in output and has largely remained unknown. Yet he is, after Dürer, Cranach, Grünewald and Altdorfer up to the time of C. D. Friedrich, the greatest painter in German art. Elsheimer's contemporaries were thoroughly aware of his "newly discovered art in painting", not only within a small circle, but principally also amongst the great persons of his age who surrendered forcibly to his effect and influence. They included Claude Lorrain, Hercules Seghers, Rubens and Rembrandt.

This new element in Elsheimer's paintings is the unity of man and landscape, of nature and creature, being close to nature, as well as his ability to indicate creative working, to represent religious reality as simply and genuinely as if it were obvious. The nocturnal expanse in our painting is not "depicted", it is comprehended in its whole infinity, actual with its deep breath, the constellations and the milky way, the full moon which illuminates the clouds around it and is reflected in the calm water.

The participation of the observer is focussed on the human and religious element by the flight of the Holy Family which takes place in front of the dark silhouette of the wood. We get the impression as if the group would move past and also past the fire which illuminates the shepherds and their animals. This impression is determined by the movement of the solid wood which, accentuated by the vibrating light of the milky way, results in a counter-rhythm to the wandering group. Although we scarcely notice it, it is not by chance that Mary is represented exactly in the centre of the picture, that the sources of light of the moon lead inwards into the picture, that Joseph illuminates the path from the back with his torch and, outside at the end of the picture completing the composition, the fire whirls its sparks into the air. This is all arranged with the greatest art and consideration, with rare abundance of feeling and meaning, of inner harmony and purity of concept.

When Rubens learnt that Elsheimer had died at the age of 32 in bitter poverty, he wrote to a joint friend: "After such a loss, our whole guild should go into deep mourning. It will not be easy to find a replacement for him and, in my opinion, there has never been one to equal him in the field of smaller figures, landscapes and so many other subjects."

16. ADAM ELSHEIMER
baptised on May 18, 1578 in Frankfort/Main, buried on December 11, 1610 in Rome.

THE FLIGHT TO EGYPT
inscribed on the back: "Adam Elsheimer fecit Romae 1609". Copper, 31 x 41 cm. Taken over from the Düsseldorf Gallery.

Giotto raised pictorial description, which had hitherto been very largely inspired by Byzantine models, to a new conception of space and of man in his physical form and in his feelings. He was therefore celebrated already in the 14th century and especially in the Renaissance as one of the great pioneers. This contemporary of Dante (who was born in Florence in 1265 and died in Ravenna in 1321) has been quite rightly described as the artist whose work ushers in the modern age.

Our conception of Giotto's style is based almost entirely on his frescoes, and in particular, the series which he painted between 1303 and 1305 in the Scrovegni chapel in the Arena at Padua. Here for the first time the human was depicted with an hitherto unknown penetration. Every episode is related with dignity and simplicity and brought to life as a vivid whole. The composition is always developed in accordance with standards and proportions acceptable to the modern mind, and permeated by an overall clarity and uniform intensity. The figures are powerful and heavy, enveloped in large and simple garments. They always give the impression of real human bodies, with their vigorous movements and strong expressiveness.

The frescoes were Giotto's most important work. Only a few panel paintings can be connected with his name. They include the Munich Crucifixion which, with two further panels in the Old Pinakothek and pictures in the Metropolitan Museum in New York, in the Gardener Collection in Boston and in the former Berenson Collection in Settigano near Florence, formed part of a predella or vestry cupboard. In the Munich Crucifixion a Franciscan monk and a pair of founders are kneeling at the foot of the Cross and mediate between the group of Mary and John. Impressive though the work is, it probably derives, like all the panel paintings associated with Giotto's name, not from the hand of the artist himself but was no doubt produced under his direct influence, by one of his immediate associates.

17. GIOTTO DI BONDONE
born about 1266 in Colle di Vespignano near Florence, died on January 8, 1337 in Florence.

CHRIST ON THE CROSS
— BETWEEN MARY AND JOHN
chestnut wood, 45 x 44 cm, acquired by King Maximilian I in 1813.

The rock fills the whole width in our small painting. The grave which is decorated at its base is carefully carved out of the bright stone, so that its black depth, equidistant from the side edges, lies in the middle of the composition and provides the serious background for the representation. There is in front of the grave a lawn interspersed with flowers, above the rock a strip of blue sky with a grey layer of cloud, at the sides a wood, the outline and mass of which answer the rhythm of the rock and the entrance to the grave as a counter-movement. There are at the edges of the picture, completely unsubstantiated by the subject, two golden pillars, as it were as a frame to stress the sacral element and effect of depth.

The figures are arranged symmetrically on this artistically rounded-off stage. They are the body of Christ which Joseph of Arimathia is supporting under the shoulders in order to lay it in the grave, Mary and John who have taken the hands of the Lord, are bowing humbly to kiss them and take their farewell. The carefully foreshortened sheet on the ground stresses the figure of the Lord as the centre of the composition, not only by its position and direction, but also by the contrast with the black of the grave. The colours match. The beautiful light blue of Mary's mantle with John's under-robe, the gentle pink of his shawl recurs in the outer-garment of Joseph of Arimathia and in Mary's robe, the shining yellow of the lining completes this simple, clear triad. The upper part of Christ's body has not yet been enveloped in the shroud. The observer is intended to see the wound on his side and recognize that this body can no longer stand, that it is a corpse and has to be supported laboriously in order to be presented for the last time to the faithful in its full appearance. It is not for nothing that we think of the veneration of the "man of sorrow".

In about 1440 Fra Giovanni painted the more than two metres high altar in the monastery of S. Marco in Florence, which had been founded by Cosimo dei Medici. The legend of the saints Cosma and Damiani, the patrons of Florence, was told in eight small pictures in the predella. It is assumed, probably correctly, that the "burial" was inserted in the centre for special veneration.

Even in his lifetime Fra Giovanni received the nickname "Angelico", the angel-like one. Passionate expressions and dramatic intensifications are foreign to his pious mind and the purity of his soul, for his religious experience and devotion spring from the depth of a lyrical feeling, the sincerity and calm of which fill his whole work. The following words are to be found on his tombstone in Santa Maria Sopra Minerva in Rome: "My fame shall not be that I was another Apelles, but that all my activity was directed to thee, Christ."

18. FRA ANGELICO
(Fra Giovanni da Fiesole), born in 1387 in Vicchio di Mugello, died in 1455 in Rome.

THE BURIAL OF CHRIST
painted in about 1440. Poplar wood, 37 x 45.5 cm. Acquired in 1818 for Crown Prince Ludwig of Bavaria.

As far as panel pictures, and not frescoes, are concerned, practically the whole of Filippo Lippi's output was devoted to the praise of the Virgin Mary. This monk of Santa Maria del Carmine was especially attracted by the subject of the Annunciation which occupied him repeatedly. He never painted the same picture twice but with his richly inventive genius was for ever creating new conceptions and new motifs, or at any rate new variants and modifications of the subject. He uses the grace and virginity, nobility and perfection of his subject to underline the religious significance of his painting. In spite of his Florentine matter-of-factness, he imbues the theme with a poetic quietness and gentleness.

In our picture, which was painted for the convent of the "Murate", the immured nuns in Florence, the scene is depicted in great detail. The humble encounter between the angel and the Virgin takes place in a motionless silence before a richly adorned, very clearly and symmetrically organised architectural structure. The refinement and restraint of the drawing is perfectly in keeping with the cool spirituality of the colour; the whole incident takes place within a supernatural reality.

19. FRA FILIPPO LIPPI
born in Florence about 1406, died in Spoleto on October 9, 1469.

THE ANNUNCIATION
poplar wood, 203 x 186 cm. Handed over from private Royal ownership to the Art Collections in 1850.

20. Botticelli
Sandro di Mariano Filipepi,
called Botticelli
*born in 1444 or 1445 in Florence,
died in Florence on May 17, 1510.*

The Lamentation over Christ
*poplar wood, 140 x 207 cm. Acquired
for Crown Prince Ludwig between
1814 and 1816, given to the State
in 1850.*

Botticelli is famous for his noble and elegant figures with their graceful gestures, for his soft, restrained colours and the cool charm of his line drawing which accorded so exactly with the refined aristocratic taste of his contemporaries. All this is forgotten and overcome in the Munich Lamentation. The scene is set in the foreground before the open tomb. It is replete with grievous tragedy and an intense feeling and passion which, for all the grandeur of the expression, remains cold. The group of the Lamentation, which is composed most impressively, seems almost as stiff and frozen as a relief. The colours are loud and hard. It is impossible to explain why the saints Hieronymus and Paul have been added on the left-hand side and St. Peter on the right. They appear in any case to have been used to fill up the stage and to relieve the drama of some of its tension. Botticelli's abandonment of his former ideals has been connected, with some justification, with the revolution in religious ideas called forth by Savonarola (1452—1498) in Florence. Botticelli was probably deeply moved by the fiery sermons in which Savonarola set the horrors of the Last Judgement before his listeners, demanded their withdrawal from all worldliness, in art as well as life, and the cultivation of piety, simplicity and asceticism. This is the only possible explanation of the style of Botticelli's few late works in which he subordinated his art to the message of this fervent Dominican monk, who in the end was burnt as a heretic.

The figure of Mary rises above a praying bench on the edge of which a black damask is spread and on which lies an open horary. There is constructed from these shapes and their colours a composition which is bold and simple, strict and economical and well-balanced with extreme certainty. The slim and, at the same time, firm hands of the mother of God which are crossed in front of her breast take up the rhythm of the open pages, lead over to her face which seems to grow out of this gesture. This oblique train of movement, which is accentuated by the brightness of the shade of the paper and of the flesh tints, gives the gentle inclination and turning of the head and the direction of the gaze its expressive determination. The peculiarly restrained and yet so intensive blue of the kerchief emerges from the black background, intensified in its effect by the modelling and concentrating significance of the light. As an essential balance within the composition, the artist has placed at the left side of the bench a red book which overlaps the edge. The picture admittedly remains restricted, but is not intended to stop here and hinder Mary's gaze and words.

The intensity of this conception creates a form of picture of great tectonic unity which seems to place itself in front of each inner utterance, as if it were independent and valid in itself. Expression and sensation lie as it were behind this strict and silent form, behind the simplifying firmness of the colour, like powerful impulses and tensions which cannot discharge themselves and precisely in that way achieve the vigorous effect of the visible.

According to an old tradition, Antonello is said to have learnt oil painting from Jan van Eyck and to have brought it to Italy where it was up till then unknown. Actually, Dutch painting technique was learnt by the young artist in Naples where Alfonso of Aragón had ruled since 1442. There were in the royal collection works by Jan van Eyck and Roger van der Weyden (see Fig. 1). It is also certain that artists from the north had settled in the city at that time. Spanish painting, which was cultivated at the court, was at this time likewise largely determined by the Netherlands.

After Antonello had returned again to Messina and had worked there for 20 years, he travelled in 1475 to Venice, but was back in his home-city again by November 1476. During this short period a series of works was created which was admired by his contemporaries and to which he gave the brilliance and sensuous force of Dutch chromaticism. Antonello became the great inspirer of Venetian painting, to whom Giovanni Bellini in particular and above him even Titian were indebted.

21. ANTONELLO DA MESSINA
born in about 1430 in Messina, died between February 14 and 25, 1479 in Messina.

MARY OF THE ANNUNCIATION
painted shortly before 1475. Walnut, 42.3 x 32.3 cm. Acquired in 1897.

"We find in the Italy of the Renaissance individual artists who create in all fields at the same time only what is new and perfect of its kind and yet who still make the greatest impression as human beings" (Jacob Burckhardt). This applies in particular to Leonardo da Vinci, the painter and sculptor, the architect, builder of fortifications and cities, the engineer and technical man, the versatile scientist and anatomist, who developed thoughts in all these fields and reached conclusions which were, often enough, to prove their validity only after centuries had past. Already at the age of 20, he was a master in Florence, but did not then establish himself independently, but remained for a further five years in the workshop of his teacher Verrocchio. It was at this time, in about 1475, that the "Madonna with the Carnation" was painted.

The maidenly Mary is standing upright behind a balustrade and is fully occupied with the child Jesus, who is grasping with lively desire at a red carnation she is handing him with a gentle, reserved movement. It is the symbol of the blood of the passion and the sacrificial death of Christ.

The foreground part of the figures is stressed, but it does not isolate them. This proximity in front of the observer and, not least, the rare omission at that time of the halos reduce the distance to the divine and stress the effect of human feelings. The natural element is desired with all inner majesty, the action is felt as present and not as permanent, as befits a devotional picture.

Near the cushion on which the child is sitting, Mary has spread out a puff of her dress on the balustrade. This drapery is arranged as an artistically beautiful creation which is valid in its own right and is such as would never result of its own accord. Local colours — shining yellow and saturated blue — form and isolate the object and give it its special significance. Next to it stands a splendid glass vase with its golden base, fitted into a shaded dusk, into the mood of the area which extends without perspective behind Mary and which is however there as atmosphere of the darkening room. In a likewise new expression, art is concentrated in the softly modelled shadow on the child's body and in the face of the Madonna, and not least in the landscape of the background which — separated and yet connected into the unity of the painting — is visible in the distance behind the high double arcades. It is freely invented, as are the flowers in the vase which cannot be identified botanically, but everything corresponds strangely to nature herself. The significance of the subdued colours with their shaping darknesses — "sfumato" — was perhaps used by Leonardo with his enquiring mind in this picture for the first time, even if not yet completely uniformly. The principle has however been found which, in its consistency, led to a new view of reality, no longer an addition of the individual, but a unity of world and life.

22. LEONARDO DA VINCI
born in 1452 at Vinci near Florence, died on May 2, 1519 at Castle Cloux near Amboise.

MADONNA WITH THE CARNATION
painted in about 1475. Poplar wood, 62 x 47 cm, cut a little at the left. Acquired in 1899.

When St. Bernard of Clairvaux, who always wanted to remain a simple monk and did so, — in his modesty he is said to have declined the bishoprics of Milan, Chartres and Spires (Speyer) —, was occupied with his homilies, the Madonna appeared to him in the company of angels. Perugino depicts the scene not as a vision, with Mary hovering over the saint, but as a silent meeting which acquires its solemnity from the quiet and calm of the figures. There is no action but one can sense them speaking very softly to each other. For their spiritual understanding, for the glances and words which pass between them, Perugino achieved a "transparency" in which the purity of the Faith is made visible. Instead of the traditional angels, two female martyrs are associated with the Madonna and two saints with St. Bernard. They act as a foil to the two main figures. The strictly symmetrical, completely balanced architecture of the portico, the view, through its central arcade, of a springtime landscape, add to the gentleness and solemnity of the atmosphere. Raphael's work was based on this noble and melodic art, with the full harmonies of its colours.

"The vision of St. Bernard" was painted circa 1490—1494 for the chapel of the Nasi family in the church of S. Maria Maddalena dei Pazzi in Florence. Between 1639 and 1647 the picture was removed from its original position; it was acquired as a legacy by the house of Capponi. A surviving copy by Felice Ficherelli, called Riposo, was put in the place in the Cappella Nasi in St. Spirito, intended for it by the testator.

23. PERUGINO
PIETRO DI CRISTOFORO VANNUCCI, called PERUGINO
born probably soon after 1450 in Città della Pieve, died in February or March 1523 in Fontignano near Perugia.

THE VISION OF ST. BERNARD
chestnut wood, 173 x 170 cm. Acquired 1829/30 for King Ludwig I.

24. RAPHAEL
RAFFAELLO SANTI DA URBINO
born probably on March 26 or 28, 1483 in Urbino, died on April 6, 1520 in Rome.

THE "MADONNA DELLA TENDA"
(with the curtain), chestnut wood, 65.8 x 51.2 cm. Acquired for Crown Prince Ludwig in 1814.

The "Madonna della Tenda" was painted in Rome circa 1513—1514 and is one of the maturest representations in the long series of approximately 40 pictures of the Virgin painted by Raphael. No other subject preoccupied him so much, apart from the frescoes destined for the Vatican and for the Villa Farnesina.

The perfection achieved by Raphael is less recognized nowadays than it was in earlier ages, since our period is seeking for almost opposite effects. In Raphael's work the form has life of its own. The colour serves the melodic line with its richness and harmony and with the haziness so typical of Raphael's mature works. The perfection of the structure is achieved by the mutual balance of all the parts, by the equilibrium of the lines, relationships and boundaries. The interplay of movement is lively, but ordered and controlled rather than direct and free, though the feeling of vitality is not thereby impaired. Raphael bestows youth and charm and divine beauty on the female figure. The type of Virgin Mary which he created, and the perfection of his art served as a model for centuries.

The "Madonna della Tenda" is probably identical with a painting which was mentioned in 1681 in a description of the Escorial. During the Napoleonic wars the picture came into private hands in England whence it was possible to acquire it for Munich.

With the victory at Mühlberg on the Elbe on April 24, 1547, Charles V had finally beaten his opponents who had joined together in the Schmalkaldic League for the defence of the Protestant faith. At the Imperial Diet which was opened at Augsburg on September 1, 1547, this success was to be consolidated by a reform of political and religious conditions in the empire. Shortly before Christmas the emperor summoned the 70 year old-old Titian, whom he had already years before appointed "Eques Caesaris", member of the imperial court and Privy Councillor, with the title of a Count Palatine and had raised to Knight of the Golden Spur, to his court residence, so that he would be available there for his commissions. At the beginning of January 1548, the prince of artists travelled with attendants and assistants to Augsburg, where he remained until October of that year. Most of the numerous portraits of the imperial family, of the most important men in the empire — also of the Elector John Frederick of Saxony, the emperor's opponent who had been brought to Augsburg as a prisoner — were destroyed in a subsequent fire. Amongst the few that were preserved is the Munich painting. Charles V, dressed in the sombre black of the Spanish court, is depicted as a sick man suffering greatly from asthma and gout, who had addressed the following words to his son Philipp in a will made in January 1548: "My weakness and the dangers of life which have scarcely been overcome make it seem advisable to give you advice in case of my death." We feel the extent to which Titian was concerned in this portrait to catch the whole nature and depth of the personality in order to depict the man who was marked by life and fate, to recognize his wisdom, mistrust, energy, hesitation and weaknesses, to include the unity as well as the discordant aspect of his character. We know from a letter from Melanchthon that Titian always had unhindered access to the emperor who a few years later abdicated voluntarily and withdrew to a lonely life in the vicinity of St. Just in Estremadura.

The special feature of this portrait does not lie solely in the value of a unique historical document, but even more in the dimension by which the representation of this physiognomy has been raised to the full truth of life. The emperor is tired, he directs his gaze resignedly towards the observer without demand and expectation. Titian's portrait of Charles V is amongst the great achievements of the European art of portraiture, irrespective of the fact that it possibly remained unfinished and was completed by another hand or that it had to be restored at an early stage because of its poor state of preservation.

25. TITIAN (TIZIANO VECELLIO) *born in Pieve di Cadore, probably in 1477, died on August 27, 1576 in Venice.*

PORTRAIT OF EMPEROR CHARLES V. *Designated on the sill:* "MDXLVIII. TITIANUS". *Canvas, 205 x 122 cm. Taken over from the Electoral Gallery in Munich.*

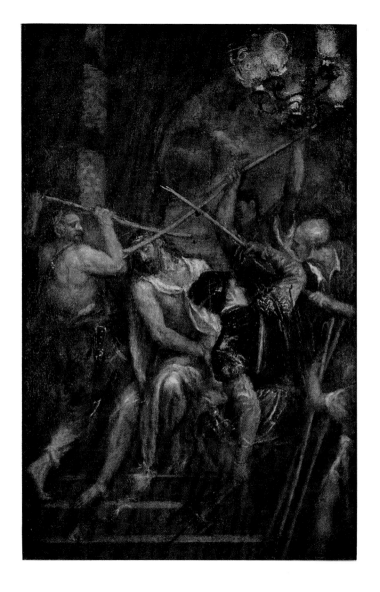

In the last years of his long life Titian reverted to the subject of the Crowning with Thorns which he had executed between 1540 and 1550 for an altar in S. Maria della Grazie in Milan (now in the Louvre). The structure and organisation of the two compositions are very similar. But in the later work the invention is no longer as essential as the depth of the artistic expression and the concentration on the meaning. What was affecting in the first version, set in a glaring light and brutal, has now become remote and mysterious. In the later version the accessories are merely hinted at. Christ does not suffer with a loud cry and with tortured eyes wide open — his eyes are closed in an attitude of quiet endurance. Dramatic movement has been replaced by submission; the episode has been monumentalised by means of introversion. The religious, it seems, has become one with the artistic in the glowing lights and the sated darkness in which the colours lose their material substance.

It is assumed that Tintoretto possessed this picture and that his son sold it to an "ultramontano", probably a Dutchman or a German. Certainly it was known to Van Dyck, as is proved by his paintings of the same subject in Berlin and Madrid.

26. TITIAN (TIZIANO VECELLIO) *born probably in 1477 in Pieve di Cadore, died in Venice on August 27, 1576.*

CHRIST CROWNED WITH THORNS *canvas, 280 x 182 cm. Before 1800 in the Court Garden Gallery in Munich.*

It was one of the great events in the history of German and European art when the prince bishop Carl Philip of Greiffenklau called the "celebre Pittor" Giovanni Battista Tiepolo from Venice to Würzburg and the master accepted the commission to decorate the Imperial Hall and the famous staircase by Balthasar Neumann in the Residence. Tiepolo arrived in Würzburg in January 1750 with his sons Giovanni Domenico and Lorenzo, who were to assist him. The work kept him in Würzburg for nearly 3 years. Apart from the extensive frescoes, which, with the later mural paintings in Venice and Madrid, represent the ultimate zenith and at the same time also the end of the development of Italian monumental painting which had ranged over several centuries, a few altar pieces were also produced during this period. Of these special mention may be made of the "Adoration of the Magi" which was executed for the Benedictine abbey of Münsterschwarzach in Franconia and is one of the principal items in Tiepolo's extraordinarily rich output. The experience of fresco technique with its relaxed method of painting and the lightness of its colour, seems to have been applied to this picture which is marked by the effect of depth in the composition and also by the free and easy application of the colour. There is also a perfect control of light and shade, a wealth of expression and a highly effective combination of organized illusion with a living actuality.

27. GIOVANNI BATTISTA TIEPOLO *born in Venice on March 5, 1696, died in Madrid on March 27, 1770.*

ADORATION OF THE MAGI *signed* GIO. B. TIEPOLO F. A. *1753, canvas, 407 x 211 cm. Transferred to the Court Garden Gallery in Munich in 1804.*

Venice spread its radiance over Europe once again in the 18th century. Next to Rome it was the most visited city, famous for its festivals and its carnival. The many foreign visitors were anxious to acquire views of the city and the demand led to an indigenous Venetian panoramic painting which, though it never occupied a leading position in the arts, enabled important masters and minor craftsmen alike to earn a living. Father Guardi already ran a Bottega (shop) for such pictures, which his son Gianantonio then took over with the assistance of his brothers Francesco and Niccoló. Apart from religious paintings, a great number of such views were produced, probably for the most part from models, and they were offered by criers on the piazza for a scudo a piece (about one half-sovereign or a quarter-eagle).

Francesco Guardi, the most outstanding of all these painters, was 70 years old when in 1782 he produced two series of festival pictures: four pictures of entertainments which the Serenissima had given for Pope Pius VI., and a further five or six of festivals in honour of the "Conti del Nord", as the Russian Grand Duke Paul Petrovich and his wife Maria Feodorovna were called. The Munich Gala Concert, which was given by pupils of music in the Sala dei Filarmonici in the old Procuratie, formed part of this series. The sparkling directness of Guardi's painterly imagination is here expressed with a glittering colourfulness which is vivified by shimmering lights. It is not surprising that in 1909 this masterpiece was recognized, and acquired, as a forerunner of Impressionism, which at that period was still far from being generally accepted.

28. FRANCESCO GUARDI
born on October 5, 1712 in Venice, died on January 1, 1793 in Venice.

GALA CONCERT IN VENICE
canvas, 68 x 91 cm, acquired in 1909.

The utopian conception of a land where work is punished, a carefree life of pleasure is rewarded and idleness esteemed as a virtue, can be traced back to the ancient world; it was also widespread in the Middle Ages. In Germany the story of the Land of Cockaigne seems to have been adopted from France in the 15th century. In 1536 a rhymed version by Hans Sachs appeared in Nuremberg. This was probably the basis of the prose version that was published in Antwerp in 1546. As many of the details coincide with Brueghel's description, it may be assumed that he knew and used this book.

In this land of gluttony three happy men have consumed to excess all the food that is freely available. Surfeited and full of good wine they have sunk down and now lie like the spokes of a wheel under the hospitable table, snoring or dreaming open-eyed, a schoolmaster or clerk, a peasant and a soldier, to all of whom the same maxim applies, perhaps as a moral warning.

What a lot of food there is here! Flans and pancakes are growing on the roof of a wooden hut. An egg, already beheaded, is hurrying along, waiting to be eaten. In the background a roasted goose offers itself appetisingly. A crisply crackling pig is waiting to be eaten, a knife already in its skin. The sausages are not actually growing on trees, but they have been intertwined to make a fence. A cactus-like plant is made up of loaves, and under a shed a roasted pigeon is shown flying into a man's mouth. Completely in the background, adjoining the sea, is the mountain of mash which a man has just eaten his way through. He is seen arriving, spoon in hand, in the blessed land.

Improbable though all this may be, nevertheless it remains closely connected with real life. Unlike the Romanists and mannerists among his contemporaries, with their over-refined style, Brueghel always keeps very close to simple everyday men, and especially to the peasant whom he loved and understood and was able, with the comprehensive power and assurance of his art, to portray in a completely new way. He depicts the people in their everyday life, in their down-to-earth matter-of-factness, vividly and truthfully, without losing himself in individual details in this newly discovered world. The freedom and unaffectedness of his creative power stand at the close of an epoch which began with the Van Eyck brothers and points the way to Rubens and Rembrandt.

29. PIETER BRUEGHEL THE ELDER *born about 1515 in the village of Brueghel near Breda, died on September 5, 1569 in Brussels.*

THE LAND OF COCKAIGNE
signed MDLXVII BRVEGEL, *oakwood, 52 x 78 cm, acquired in 1917.*

Jan Brueghel the Elder, a son of Pieter Brueghel the Elder (see Fig. 29) was, in common with his father, known and honoured throughout Europe because of his numerous small landscapes with their rich array of figures, because of his allegories and, not least, because of his "flower pieces". He received the title of a "Painter of the Governor of the Netherlands", an honour he shared with Rubens alone.

In this present painting, a large bunch of flowers, almost a metre in height, is arranged artistically in a wooden tub. Over the edge of the tub there is an abundance of smaller flowers and berries, above them roses and tulips, closely packed together with small flowers and finally, higher up before the green of copious leaves, irises, a madonna lily, a fritillaria and a peony. There are on the table, as if by chance, a fallen branch with blackberries, a small leaf and a cyclamen with small roots. Butterflies have settled here and there, as well as amongst the other flowers, a cockchafer runs over the table and a dragon-fly holds onto the edge of the tub.

In the contemporary description of such a flower piece the "grandezza", charm, extreme effort, accuracy and fineness of the execution are stressed just as much as the complete trueness to nature of the representation. The flower is not treated as a botanical object, but as a "jewel of nature" which the painter as well as the observer want to capture in all its details and as if under a magnifying glass. Brueghel developed a well-devised, skilful and masterly style of painting in this exactness of reproduction after the manner of a miniature.

He constructs his composition in a very considered arrangement, in which each flower and leaf preserves its independance and is also depicted "completely" and as being of equal value. The multiplicity has been united to an architecture of the manifold, but not combined to powerful liveliness. And even if each plant has been painted according to nature, everything has seemingly been brought together and collected effortlessly, because this flower blossoms in the spring, but that one not until summer or early autumn. We want distinctness and find it not only in the formal diffusion, but also in the balanced, clear colour which is applied transparently with fine nuances and models the shape with a light and supple tinge of light or shade. This painting corresponded to the taste of Brueghel's contemporaries and could even stand its. ground alongside the brilliant works of Rubens who often sought his friend's co-operation if flowers were to be introduced into his pictures. Rubens also painted the portrait for the tombstone of his friend and wrote his epitaph.

30. JAN BRUEGHEL THE ELDER
born in 1568 in Brussels, died January 12, 1625 in Antwerp.

FLOWER PIECE
painted towards 1610. Oak, 125.5 by 96 cm. Taken over from the Düsseldorf Gallery.

When Rubens travelled to Antwerp on October 28, 1608 precipitately from Italy to see his seriously ill mother once again, he had been in the service of the Duke of Mantua for more than eight years. He had adapted himself to aristocratic courtly life, had been in almost all the large cities of Italy, had on behalf of his master accompanied a delegation to the emperor in Spain, had saturated himself with ancient art and learning, had absorbed from the works of his contemporaries and predecessors what appealed to him, had painted many altars and numerous portraits and had acquired a name and fame virtually second to none. His mother was no longer alive when he arrived. He withdrew himself in his sorrow for a prolonged period and was undecided as to whether he should return to Italy or remain in Antwerp, where he was appointed court painter under particularly good conditions in order to keep him there. The solution came through his marriage to the 18 year-old Isabella Brant, the daughter of the respected Antwerp town-clerk. Rubens married her on October 13, 1609.

The life-size portrait of the couple was painted in the following year. The figures fill it almost to the edge in order to give life its full presence and proximity. They are sitting in the open air, Isabella probably on a cushion, lower than her husband, sheltered in the dark of a honeysuckle bower with its symbolical meaning of "the-longer-the-dearer" and protected by her husband who sits above and somewhat behind her, the landscape on the side indicates the view into the world. The dress of the couple is princely, Rubens having chosen restrained colours for himself which fit into the harmony as deeper shades. As the figures incline towards one another and their hands rest gently and as a matter of course in one another, their gazes also slip away from the world of phenomena and confirm in their contentment to the observer the certainty of such a union. An inner movement determines the various details of the composition, gives the rhythms the expression of human fellowship, places the colours and the light in the service of this balanced harmony. The simple and undeliberate nature of the attitude is determined by the highest art, which has kept everything that is private and fortuitous away from this masterpiece and, without any pathos, as if out of itself, can express the higher order and call of marital solidarity. Rubens himself once said that it was in the portrait a matter of "the reflection of the spiritual".

31. PETER PAUL RUBENS
born June 28, 1577 in Siegen (Westphalia), died May 30, 1640 in Antwerp.

RUBENS AND ISABELLA BRANT
in the honeysuckle bower. Painted in 1610. Canvas, 178 x 136 cm. Taken over from the Düsseldorf Gallery.

32. PETER PAUL RUBENS
*born on June 28, 1577 in Siegen
(Westphalia), died on May 30, 1640
in Antwerp.*

HÉLÈNE FOURMENT
*oakwood, 164 x 136 cm, acquired by
Elector Max Emanuel of Bavaria in
1698.*

Rubens married for the second time on December 6, 1630 and soon afterwards painted his young wife Hélène Fourment who was not yet 17 years old. He himself was 53. He had travelled through much of Europe, was a court painter and so overwhelmed with commissions that he had to maintain a large workshop in order to fulfil them. He was famous and well-to-do, one of the most esteemed and admired of artists, an excellent society man who was entrusted with diplomatic missions and negotiations by his masters. It has been suggested that our portrait is a wedding picture. Rubens certainly imbued it with the deep affection which flowed form this new and extremely happy union, but he was also determined to make an impressive show. He put his young wife in a castle-like setting, and in front of rich drapery, showing her in a precious gown, with sumptuous jewels, as though she were a queen. Stimulated by the speaking presence of her being, and informed by the utter freshness and immediacy of the masterly painting, such as Rubens alone could have produced, he achieved a work from which he never parted. It was one of his most important human and artistic possessions.

In the inventory of Rubens' estate this picture is described thus: "Un berger caressant sa bergère" (a shepherd caressing his shepherdess). It is a late work, later than 1635, the theme of which was probably prompted by personal experiences and ideas, and transferred to an imaginary setting. A half-naked shepherd, with whom, though it is not actually a self-portrait, Rubens probably identified himself, is making ardent advances to a young woman who resembles Hélène Fourment. Though she is fighting against his attempt to embrace her, there is something in her expression which suggests that consent is only just around the corner. The incident takes place in the open air. A mountain spring is indicated and one imagines the shepherd singing somewhere near a little while before or playing on his bagpipes before he caught sight of the woman and felt a desire to approach her.

Everything is seen quite close up and is shown happening at this very moment. To quote from Jacob Burckhardt: "Rubens knew quite certainly that what is not immediately advantageous to the moment, impairs it". All his figures "somehow live in the moment and the moment in them". The marvel of this painting lies not only in its natural strength, its nobility, its inexhaustible wealth and superabundant fullness, but equally in the inner mastery and control with which Rubens permeates his art.

33. PETER PAUL RUBENS
born on June 28, 1577 in Siegen (Westphalia), died on May 30, 1640 in Antwerp.

PASTORAL SCENE
oakwood, 162 x 134 cm. From the Mannheim Gallery.

34. SIR ANTHONY VAN DYCK
(VAN DYKE)
born on March 22, 1599 in Ant-
werp, died on December 9, 1641 in
Blackfriars (London).

Presumably PORTRAIT OF THE
BATTLE PAINTER PEETER SNAYERS
(1592—1666), oakwood, 29 x 21 cm;
from the Mannheim Gallery.

Van Dyck, the son of wealthy parents and blessed with a precocious talent, so that he received the freedom of his guild before he was 19, was the most important pupil of Rubens, in whose studio he worked until he was 22 or 23. There followed a longish stay in Italy. After that Van Dyck was in Antwerp and also in Holland. In 1632 he moved to London where he became court painter to Charles I and lived there with few interruptions until his death.

This brilliant career was crowned with successes which he achieved with religious works but mainly with portraits. Van Dyck was *the* portrait painter of his generation. With his lively mind and light touch he achieved such excellent likenesses that he soon became the favourite artist of high society. He was concerned with the grand style in portrait painting, with capturing the obviously characteristic qualities of his subjects rather than plumbing their spiritual depths. Above all he strove to portray the living personality, the outward style and the social ambience. What is presumed to be a portrait of the battle painter Snayers was certainly not a commissioned work: it was done for a friend, who in the portrait has raised his head and eyes somewhat haughtily, and displays a certain arrogance with a turn of the mouth and an expression in the eyes. This showing-off attitude is presented as something very personal and reproduced with the assurance of a great and mature master.

The 16 year-old Adriaen Brouwer migrated from the Flemish Oudenaarde where he was born to Holland. It is probable that he ran away from home. He lived and painted in Holland, mainly in Haarlem, where he certainly began as a pupil of Frans Hals and achieved recognition and fame in a very short time. It is not known why Brouwer returned in 1631 to the South that was under Spanish occupation and settled in Antwerp.

Brouwer was a man who led his life without any regard for society. He was unrestrainedly addicted to alcohol and tobacco, frequented the lowest inns, was constantly heavily in debt and always stating, even before the courts, that he would recompense his creditors with pictures. People accepted this, for his work was so much in demand that even during his lifetime copies by others and forgeries were on the market. Brouwer died at the age of 32. We do not know whether it was from the plague or as a result of his excesses, for brandy and tobacco were at that time dangerous narcotics because of their method of preparation.

The cheap inn was his milieu which he depicted originally and realistically, with peasants and beggars, drinking and smoking, playing and fighting, at feasts, at slaughterings, and elsewhere, always however outside their real occupation and daily toil. Brouwer mirrors his own experiences, his being why his artistic touch always grasps what is genuine, true to nature and in all its ugliness. It is for this reason that his figures always strike us as being so obvious and convincing, even after the manner of portraits, although they were certainly not painted from life. The mimic expression and the action are stressed, but subordinated to the anecdotal nature of the story. He sees this his world as he does himself, not without irony and also not without a certain humour. Decisive for him is nevertheless the protest against the art of the church and of the aristocracy with its need for pathos and large-scale representation. Sandrart called him in 1675, not without justification, a "Diogenese cynicus". Brouwer admittedly did not tackle any new subject with his paintings of peasants, but did however coin a type of picture which virtually started with him and continued to exist for a long time in Flemish and Dutch painting.

The high regard which Brouwer's contemporaries had for his art is clear from the fact that Rubens, who always championed him, possessed no fewer than seventeen paintings by him, while Rembrandt had eight. To his posthumous fame, the Old Pinakothek shows in a "Brouwer Cabinet" the largest collection of his paintings which exists today.

35. ADRIAEN BROUWER
born between 1605 and 1606 in Oudenaarde, buried February 1, 1638 in Antwerp.

SMOKING AND DRINKING PEASANTS IN AN INN
Probably painted in about 1635. Oil on wood, 35 x 26 cm. Taken over from the Hofgarten Gallery.

Throughout his life Frans Hals only painted portraits, for even his popular figure and genre paintings were conceived as portraits. Unlike the cosmopolitan Van Dyck, he lived in the middle-class society of Haarlem, portraying the councillors and preachers, the merchants and artisans with their wives, and also the officers of the rifle associations which evolved from the guilds.

No details are known about Mynheer Croes and yet from the portrait we know at once that he was a jovial, portly Dutchmann, a strong man fond of eating much and well and not averse to a well-filled glass. This much is revealed not only by the "speaking" likeness but equally by the artistic interpretation which Frans Hals has added to the physical likeness: his uncomplicated conception of man whom he always brings into a direct relationship with the beholder. He gives the picture an immediacy which is enhanced by the expression. The painting itself is equally direct. The product of a few hours and a free application of the colours, it shows a control and a technical ease and assurance which even Van Dyck admired. Arnold Houbraken (1660 till 1719) has recorded in his "Groote Schouburgh der Nederlandsche Konstschilders en -schilderessen" (1718—1721) that Van Dyck declared that he had never known anyone who had the paintbrush so much in his power as Frans Hals, who, when he had planned a portrait, knew how to reproduce the essential characteristics in the right place with a single stroke of the brush and without having to alter anything. He applied the colours thick and well-blended, then added the broad strokes of the brush, saying: "Now the painter's handwriting must go in!"

36. FRANS HALS
born probably in 1580 in Antwerp, died on August 29, 1666 in Haarlem.

PORTRAIT OF WILLEM CROES
signed with the monogram F. H., oakwood, 47 x 34 cm, acquired in 1906.

The view of the choir ambulatory of St. James' in Utrecht is reproduced with archaeological exactitude and fidelity and yet there is none of the dryness and painfully pedantic carefullness which is usually inseparable from this kind of thoroughness. On the contrary: it is the true greatness of the architecture which is reproduced in this careful description. Furthermore, the space, not the mere spatial structure, is depicted, and the light that fills it and animates with its silent effects the sober walls and columns. Unlike other specialists in Dutch architectural painting, Saenredam introduces only a very few accessory figures into his pictures; he was not interested in the people in the church or in public worship, but rather in the life of the lucid and sober Protestant interior, its quietness and its breath. With what graceful precision he follows the manifold transitions from light to shade! He seems to catch their essential momentariness. Yet he never painted on the spot. He first made careful drawings and then executed the painting itself in his Haarlem studio, with the aid of an extraordinary memory for light conditions and light values. Judging by the few pictures that have survived, Saenredam seems to have worked very slowly and very carefully. His quiet retiring art is one of the noblest and most characteristic achievements of Dutch painting.

37. PIETER JANSZ(OON) SAENREDAM
born on June 9, 1597 in Assendelft, buried in Haarlem on May 31, 1665.

VIEW OF THE CHOIR AMBULATORY OF ST. JAMES' CHURCH IN UTRECHT *signed: "Pieter Sardam im Jaer 1642", oakwood, 55.2 x 43.7 cm; from the prince-bishop's gallery in Würzburg.*

No artist ever painted, drew, or etched so many self-portraits as Rembrandt. The sequence reflects the fortunes and misfortunes of his life like a never-ceasing report on himself, in which, without any attempt at extenuation, everything is recorded that has touched and moved the artist, little happiness and joy, much hardship and disappointment, pain and patient expectation. He was 23 when he painted our little picture in which he depicts himself confronting life with urgent and uncertain questionings. The violence of the questioning is expressed in the vainly searching eyes and in the lips which seem to be demanding an answer.

In any attempt to analyse the artistic methods employed the first thing that strikes one is the treatment of the light, the biggest emphasis being placed on the white lace collars, with only the right cheek and the nose illuminated besides. The forehead and the eyes are fighting their way out of a murky darkness in a dramatic encounter which underlines the uncertainty and doubt. The tension is also increased by the energy with which the shoulder, which is also in the light, thrusts itself into the picture. The directness of the utterance is also accented by the density of the picture. A man can only portray his own self thus, out of his own suffering: no other person could possibly see inside him so profoundly.

38. Rembrandt Harmensz(oon) van Rijn
born on July 15, 1606 in Leiden, died on October 8, 1669 in Amsterdam.

Self-Portrait as a Youth
oakwood 15.6 x 12.7 cm. Acquired in 1953.

From 1633 to 1639 Rembrandt painted for Prince Frederick Hendrick of Orange a series of five pictures of the Passion (in the Old Pinakothek), the only commission which he received from a prince in his life. Although it was executed later and without any relationship to the other paintings, the "Adoration of the shepherds" was, on account of its subject and similar size, added to this series which was already in the Düsseldorf Gallery about 1700 and came thence to Munich at the beginning of the 19th century.

The chosen scene is a farmhouse that may be imagined somewhere on the Dutch plain without the gates of Amsterdam. The shepherds and Mary and Joseph are such everyday figures that one might easily meet them at the nearest market. One observes only on closer inspection that the light gathered in the darkness does not proceed from a natural source but radiates as it were supernaturally from the Christ child, mysteriously illuminating the figures and faces; its effect is further intensified by the contrast of the rear figure in the foreground. In this as it were living light the setting seems indefinite, yet remarkably close and real. Unpretentiously though the religious theme is presented, there is a deep sense of the universal humanity which makes the divine understandable. With the inner truth of his religious representations Rembrandt comes very close to the words of the Gospel, which he realizes rather than merely interprets.

39. REMBRANDT HARMENSZ(OON) VAN RIJN
born on July 15, 1606 in Leiden, died on October 8, 1669 in Amsterdam.

THE ADORATION OF THE SHEPHERDS
signed: . . . ndt f. 1646; canvas, 98 x 72 cm; from the Düsseldorf Gallery.

In the development of Dutch painting in the 17th century special types evolved such as the portrait, the genre-picture, the still life, the animal picture, the sea picture and other special subjects on which particular artists concentrated. As far as landscape is concerned, Jacob van Ruisdael was probably the best known and most widely esteemed "specialist"

In order to paint our picture he climbed up on to a slight eminence. He shows us the wide plain with its low horizon in the far distance. A village lies with its roofs embedded in trees and fields; the corn has just been cut; sheep are grazing on a field that has just been harvested. The perpendicular line of the church tower is sharply accented. Over this landscape there lies a lofty sky with great clouds drifting in the sea wind. They bring about a constant change of light and shade, an enlivening interplay of light and dark in the picture. Earth and sky are united by this wealth of light and its variety.

Ruisdael, who painted his pictures in the studio, not in the open air itself, always keeps close to Nature, which he confronts with a penetrating understanding. He in particular discovered an artistic characterisation for the Dutch landscape, for its peculiar quietness and atmosphere, which was never attained again and which over the centuries has retained its importance and its exemplary quality.

40. JACOB VAN RUISDAEL
born in Haarlem in 1628 or 1629, buried on March 14, 1682 in Haarlem.

THE DUNES
canvas, 59 x 73 cm, acquired in 1942.

What the trumpeter in his elegant costume has to convey to his master's lady in a letter, and how she receives the message, the contents of which she does not yet know — all this accords with the presuppositions of genre painting. Ter Borch was fond of choosing such subjects, sometimes with a single figure, sometimes with groups. He varies the same motifs, as agreeable as they are unimportant, and always takes them from the middle-class milieu in which the buyers of his pictures lived.

It is very noticeable to what an extent these scenes revolve around the persons and how unexpressive are the actual interiors. The elegant rooms are often only indicated with a dim tone which conveys the illusion of a quiet space. The content was certainly not without significance for Ter Borch, but at the same time and to a large extent it was merely the pretext for a painting of supreme refinement and richly differentiated colouring. Ter Borch was already famous in his own lifetime for his reproduction of velvet and silk and other materials, but the virtuosity of his technique was not the important thing, rather the mystery that is inherent in the perfection of such painting.

41. GERARD TER BORCH
born in Zwolle at the end of 1617, died on December 8, 1681 in Deventer.

THE LETTER
signed: G. T. Borch, oakwood, 56 by 46 cm; mentioned as in Castle Schleissheim in 1781.

91

42. Nicolas Poussin
*born in Villers nears Les Andelys
in Normandy in June 1594, died on
November 19, 1665 in Rome.*

Midas and Bacchus
*canvas, 98 x 134.5 cm; in Castle
Nymphenburg in 1781.*

Midas, a mythical king in Phrygia has just, during a feast, decided a competition in flute playing for Bacchus and against Apollo, and in our picture Apollo is indignantly contesting the verdict. According to the legend, he punished Midas by making him grow the ears of an ass, which he kept hidden under a tall "Phrygian" cap. Only a servant knew the secret, which he confided to a lake when he was no longer able to keep it to himself. At once there shot up from the damp ground reeds which henceforth whispered the secret to anyone who wished to hear it.

In a letter to Rubens of July 1631 a "King Midas" by Poussin is mentioned as having been sold. This was presumably our picture. If so, it was painted circa 1630, in the first zenith of Poussin's Roman development.

As in the French theatre it is the suprapersonal order that the artist seeks, such as is only provided in large and important subjects. According to Poussin himself, the artist must endeavour "to keep away from all trivialities, with all the strength at his command, so as not to impair the sublime dignity of the story". He must not only be able "to shape the material, but also have the discernment to recognize and understand it, and he must always select it so that it is naturally suitable for any kind of adornment and for perfection". Beauty arises from the harmony of order and measure with form and colour, which must correspond in a clear and balanced accord. There is no place for trivial human feelings in the epic language of such art. Its high intellectual level implies a form of perfect beauty and reason, and demands that art must rise above mere nature.

For Claude Lorrain the landscape is a revelation by the Creator of the eternal. Hence nature is purified and seen in mythical grandeur. Claude seeks for its inner ordering, for its structural laws and thereby bestows on it the solemnity and greatness of the sublime. In this respect the Roman landscape was ideal.

Man is set in such surroundings without giving them a purpose or impairing their rational clarity. Man is not merely an accessory, he is not without meaning, through him the measure of Nature's independence and inner greatness is emphasized. The repudiation of Hagar and her son Ishmael by Abraham (Genesis 21) is not a violent action, but a just and worthy procedure, the significance of which is also underlined by its actual content.

This art seeks for the measured and also for the measurable. It develops its compositions with the utmost clarity without ever succumbing to convention. The colours are used firmly but with restraint, perfectly adapted to the harmonious atmosphere of the light that transfigures Claude's landscapes with a calm and wideness peculiar to him alone.

The Old Pinakothek possesses a counterpart to this picture, "Hagar and Ishmael in the Wilderness", which has from an early period also been called "Afternoon Landscape", which shows how much the description of Nature was set above the content of the picture.

43. CLAUDE GELÉE,
called CLAUDE (LE) LORRAIN
born in 1600 in Chamagne near Mirecourt on the Moselle, died in Rome on November 23, 1682.

THE REPUDIATION OF HAGAR
("MORNING LANDSCAPE")
signed: Claude Gelle Roma 1668, canvas, 106 x 140 cm; from the Palatinate-Zweibrücken Gallery in Carlsberg Castle near Homburg on the Saar.

At the same period as Watteau was producing his courtly "Fêtes galantes" (Gallant Fêtes) and Boucher his elegant shepherd scenes and mythologies, Chardin was painting his still lifes. They are no sumptuous arrangements but fruits, as it were painted for their own sake and in their plain simplicity, merely from a need to pursue their colour effects and put them in a picture. Like these fruits his figures are also committed to a "still" life. They are not naked goddesses and nymphs, or elegant society ladies, but simple folk, girls and women working in the kitchen, and occasionally a boy amusing himself blowing soap bubbles or building a house of cards.

There is no question of "social accusation" in these pictures, since in this choice of subject there is no more "preparation" for the French Revolution than in the melancholy with which Watteau expresses the transitory in all his festive scenes.

Chardin shows his people not at their work but as it were outside their ordinary activity. Our kitchen-maid, for example, moved by other thoughts and feelings, is resting her hands and occupied with herself, gazing aimlessly into the distance. It is this inner quietness that gives the composition and the colour effect its harmonious and genuine sound. It is true that the colour typifies the subject, analysing its subtlest nuances, but it is used more significantly for its own sake than for its descriptive function. For this reason Chardin has rightly been called a forerunner of Cézanne.

Incidentally, the fact that Chardin repeated his pictures and returned in later life to earlier themes also shows that he was not particularly interested in the subject-matter as such. For an example we have our "Woman cleaning Turnips", of which three further copies are extant, one in Frederick the Great's gallery in Sanssouci, another was formerly owned by the Prince of Liechtenstein and is now in the National Gallery in Ottawa, and a third somewhat modified version is in private ownership in Paris. Like our picture, all these can be traced back to the 18th century and almost to the artist's studio. They were done in fulfilment of orders for what was apparently a very popular subject.

44. JEAN-BAPTISTE
SIMÉON CHARDIN
born on November 2, 1699 in Paris,
died on December 6, 1779 in Paris.

WOMAN CLEANING TURNIPS
signed: Chardin, canvas, 46 x 37 cm.
From the Palatinate-Zweibrücken
Gallery in Carlsberg Castle near
Homburg on the Saar.

Boucher was the "First Painter" of King Louis XV of France. He knew better than anyone else how to reproduce the charm, courtly playfulness and sensuality that the age desired. The pastoral scenes are his world, with their dallying and their grace, their freedom from care and their erotic intimations. The subjects from antiquity were also chosen from this angle and with regard to their physical attractiveness, no matter whether the stories were concerned with Venus or Diana, or the rape of Europa, or "merely" with bathing nymphs. The demand for Boucher's paintings shows how greatly he was esteemed; to meet the demand he set up a workshop where he had much of his work executed and often copied for further sales. There are, for example, several versions of the "Reclining Girl", the picture in the Old Pinakothek being the final version which Boucher executed entirely with his own hand. It is at the same time probably the most famous. Only he was able to paint in this way the softness of a girl's body, its tender and youthful freshness, the gleam of the blossoming skin, the readiness for sensual experience and at the same time the expression of innocence. Thus he did justice to the aesthetic ideal of his time.

The English painter Reynolds records visiting Boucher in his studio and learning that he never worked from nature. Preserved from taking over any naturalistic details, he thereby attained the uniform idealisation of his figures and the perfect unity of his pictures. Since, however, the "Reclining Girl" is known by the name Miss Louise O'Murphy, it might be thought that she served as a model for her portrait. But in fact the picture arose, like all the others, from the artist's own imagination. The young lady's pose is only apparently a natural one; in reality it has been composed with much thought and cunning, no less than the seemingly accidental confusion of the drapery which has been brought with great deliberation into harmony with the still life on the floor and blends in colourfully with the whole picture.

45. François Boucher
born on September 29, 1703 in Paris, died on May 30, 1770 in Paris.

Reclining Girl
signed bottom left: F. Boucher 1752, canvas, 59 x 73 cm. From the Palatinate-Zweibrücken Gallery in Carlsberg Castle near Homburg on the Saar.

Greco was completely forgotten during the 18th and 19th centuries and was only rediscovered when the "Fauves" in France and the "Expressionists" in Germany began to make headway with their new vision of the world, recognizing that the "deformation" of the pattern of Nature and colour liberated from the characterisation of the subject are able to intensify the expression. Greco, the painter of "unheard of degeneration", became the "prophet of modern art".

Greco had absorbed the tradition of Byzantine art when he became a pupil of Titian in Venice, but he was also influenced by the art of Bassano, Tintoretto and Veronese. He then lived for some time in Rome, decided to go to Spain and in the spring of 1577 arrived in Toledo, where he stayed to the end of his life. The first big commission in his new homeland was a "Stripping of Christ", which is still preserved in the main vestry of the cathedral. There are several extant smaller size repetitions of this work, the most important of which is in the Old Pinakothek.

Christ, the only full-length figure, stands in the centre of the scene in the restless surging throng of myrmidons, servants and spectators, not only outstanding compositionally but also by the splendidly shining colour of his robe and by his calm amid the uproar. He alone raises his eyes from earth to heaven. Everything serves to glorify Him, the half-length figures of the three Marys in their grief, and also the brutal fellows who are tormenting Him, tearing the mantle from his body and boring the holes for the nails in the cross. They too serve, by way of spiritual contrast, to underline the Christian message of the scene. The Captain in his Spanish armour — evidently a portrait, it may even be of the artist himself, — belongs to our world and looks knowingly at the beholder.

46. EL GRECO
DOMENICO THEOTOKOPULI,
called EL GRECO (THE GREEK)
born in 1541 allegedly in Candia in Crete, died on April 7, 1614 in Toledo.

THE STRIPPING OF CHRIST
canvas 165 x 99 cm, acquired in 1909.

Our portrait of a young man who, to judge by his dress, was a member of the court of Philip IV, was painted circa 1629, shortly before the artist's Italian journey. At that time Velázquez had already been working as a court painter for some years and had met Rubens whom great commissions had taken to Madrid. His position as "Royal portraitist" and also his personal inclination led to his special preoccupation with the portrait and to his repeatedly painting the King and the Royal family in ever new guises, with perfect fidelity to the subject and a magnificently official approach that allowed no room for any private feelings. How greatly the King esteemed his painter is shown by the fact that he had one of his equestrian portraits exhibited publicly on the front steps of San Felipe, which was the more remarkable in that exhibitions in the modern sense were at that period still quite unknown.

Velázquez does not idealize his subjects. He tries to capture the reality of life itself in the picture and thus to preserve it from all the assaults of fate. He is always concerned with people, which is why he hardly ever treated religious subjects. Unmistakable though the completely personal and supremely masterly handwriting is, the artist withdraws himself and his own feelings from the picture, leaving his subject alone with the beholder. In our portrait, which, for some reason, was never finished, the speaking expression and the noble attitude are instict with pulsing actuality, as is also the direct language of the painting with its magnificent black in which Velázquez has never been surpassed. It is not surprising to learn that he had a strong influence on Manet and thereby on the beginnings of modern art.

47. VELÁZQUEZ
DIEGO RODRIGUEZ
DE SILVA Y VELÁZQUEZ
*baptised on June 6, 1599 in Seville,
died on August 6, 1660 in Madrid.*

PORTRAIT OF A YOUNG SPANIARD
*canvas, 89.5 x 69.5 cm; from the
Düsseldorf Gallery.*

Murillo, who was always preoccupied with religious motifs, depicted in some of his genre pictures the real world of the models he used for his angels; street-arabs trying their hands at business, gambling away their meagre earnings at dice, or having something to eat. Understandably, these delightful works became very popular, especially abroad, which is why nearly all these paintings are now to be found outside Spain, and the five best known in the Old Pinakothek.

In a way that is very typical of Spanish art the precisely observed reality is combined with an idealising feeling, and the aim of depicting an actual scene with a very deliberate pictorial construction in which the incident is arranged with a view to the utmost clarity. Murillo's genre pictures are notable for their lack of moralising tendencies. He wants to show the street-arabs just as he has observed them, in the tattered clothes in which they romp about the streets and market places, since he is concerned with objectivity and truthfulness, as understood by his age. Today the carefree lads seem to us to have been somewhat prettified. The artistic achievement is therefore all the more remarkable: the compositional concentration on the dice-throwing and the number-counting, not only in the gestures and miming but also in the distribution of the masses and lines, in the weight and tones of the colours. Then there is also the secondary motif, the standing boy with the dog who will certainly get a piece of his master's bread: this serves as a prelude and contrast to the main subject. This little figure and the look in its eyes invite the beholder not to pass by; true, he is not thereby implicated in the scene but it does make him feel the aliveness of it.

48. BARTOLOMÉ ESTÉBAN MURILLO *baptised on January 1, 1618 in Seville, died on April 3, 1682 in Seville.*

BEGGAR BOYS THROWING DICE *canvas, 146 x 108 cm; acquired in 1698 through the Elector Max Emanuel.*

INDEX